a northern alphabet

Arctic Beaver Cabin Drums Eagle Fire Geese Husky Igloo Jackrabbit Kayak Loon Muskeg North Owl Pack Quill

Aa Bb Cc Dd Ee Ff Gg Hh Ii Jj Kk Ll Mm Nn Oo Pp Qq Rr Ss Tt Uu Vv Ww Xx Yy Zz

Dedicated to William Hamilton of Swan Hills,
Alberta and all the children north of sixty.

Copyright © 1982 by Ted Harrison

Published in Canada by Tundra Books,
75 Sherbourne Street, Toronto, Ontario M5A 2P9

Published in the United States by Tundra Books of Northern New York,
P.O. Box 1030, Plattsburgh, New York 12901

Library of Congress Catalog Number: 82-50244

We acknowledge the support of the Canada Council for the Arts
for our publishing program. We acknowledge the financial support
of the Government of Canada through the Book Publishing Industry
Development Program (BPIDP) and that of the Government
of Ontario through the Ontario Media Development Corporation's
Ontario Book Initiative.

Awards:
Choice Book, Children's Book Centre, Toronto, 1982
IBBY Honor List, 1984
Selectors' Choice, Bro-dart Elementary School Library Collection, 1985
Biennale Illustrations in Bratislava, 1985

Printed in China

10 11 12 13 14   10 09 08 07 06

Library and Archives Canada Cataloguing in Publication

Harrison, Ted, 1926–
    A northern alphabet

ISBN-10: 0-88776-233-6 ISBN-13: 978-0-88776-233-8

1. English language – Alphabet – Juvenile literature.
I. Title.

PS8565.A658N67 2000   j421'.1   C89-090128-7
PZ7.H37No 2000

Raven Snow Trout Uniform Valley Walrus Xmas Yukon Zipper Alaska Bear Canada Dancers Ermine Forest Game

Arctic Beaver Cabin Drums Eagle Fire Geese Husky Igloo Jackrabbit Kayak Loon Muskeg North Owl Pack Quill

Aa Bb Cc Dd Ee Ff Gg Hh Ii Jj Kk Ll Mm Nn Oo Pp Qq Rr Ss Tt Uu Vv Ww Xx Yy Zz

a northern alphabet

by Ted Harrison

Tundra Books

Raven Snow Trout Uniform Valley Walrus Xmas Yukon Zipper Alaska Bear Canada Dancers Ermine Forest Game

This is an alphabet book. But it is also a puzzle book, a story book and a games book.

The North is full of interest. The names of some of its people, places, animals and objects are mentioned under each letter. How many more can you find in the paintings? If you need some help, turn to the back of the book.

Every picture is also the beginning of a story. Can you make up the rest of the story to tell yourself and your friends?

And if you like to play games, see how many words—not just nouns, but also verbs, adjectives and adverbs—you can put into your story using the letter on the page. Take the letter T for instance. The story starts: Trapper Tom has three frozen trout. You might continue: He tripped over his toboggan as he was tramping through the snow to his trapline. What happened next?

Have fun.

Ted Harrison   Whitehorse, The Yukon

Aa

Alex lives
in the **Arctic.**
He is wearing an
anorak.

Braeburn

Belcher Islands

Burwash Landing

Bylot

Back River

Babine

Buffalo Narrows

Bb

Brenda and
Billy are
being chased by a
bear.

Cc

Above the **cabin**
flies the
flag of
Canada.

Dd

The **ducks**
watch the
children do a
dance.

Ee

Eric is wearing **earmuffs.** He sees the **electric lights.**

Fairbanks Fort Smith Fort McPherson Faro Frobisher Bay Franklin Fort Hope Fort Liard Forty Mile Fullerton Frances Lake

Fond-du-Lac

Fort Nelson

Fort Good Hope

Fort Severn

Fort Chimo

Forty Mile

Faro

Fort Collinson Fort George Fort Vermilion Fort St. John Fort Chimo Fort Severn Fort Good Hope Fort Nelson Fond-du-Lac

Ff

The **frypan** will soon fry **fish** on the **flames.**

Gg

Georgie
is greeting
his **grandmother.**

Henrietta Maria
High Prairie
Hopedale
Hebron
Hayes River
Haakon Fiord
Hubbard

Hh

The **husky** is watching the boys play **hockey**.

Ii

The **Inuit** children are interested in a new **igloo**.

Jj

Joe
and **Jenny**
dance a
jig.

Kk

Kate and
Kevin are
kissing behind the
kayak.

Labrador   Lake Harbour   Lower Post   Lac à l'Eau-Claire   Lake Laberge   Labyrinth Bay   La Loche   Leaf Rapids   Lynn Lake

Lake Minchumina

Labyrinth Bay

Llewellyn Glacier

Lesser Slave Lake

Livingstone

L l

The lonely **loon** floats past the **lemming.**

Laderoute Lake   Lancaster Sound   Lansing River   Little Salmon   Little Teslin Lake   Liard River   Lac la Ronge   Lake Minchumina

Mackenzie   Mount McKinley   Melville Island   Mayo   McLennan   Menihek Lakes   Manitoba   Minto   Mara River   Marsh Lake

Mm

Mary runs by
a **moose**
munching in the
muskeg.

MacAlpine Lake

MacInnis Lake

Maclean Strait

Manitung Island

Mara River

Mayo

MacAlpine Lake   MacInnis Lake   Maclean Strait   Maud Bight   McClure Strait   McClintock Channel   Mansel Island   Mount Logan

Nn

The **northern lights**
shine
in the sky at
night.

Oo

The **owl**
can see the
oilrig from the
outhouse.

Pp

The man in the red
parka
is passing the
paddlewheeler.

Quebec   Queen Charlotte Islands   Quartz Lake   Queen Elizabeth   Queen Maud Gulf   Queens Channel   Quiet Lake   Quoich River

Qq

Mother is quietly making a quilt.

Queen Maud Gulf   Queens Channel   Quiet Lake   Quoich River   Quunnguq Lake

Quiet Lake   Quunnguq Lake   Quill Creek   Lac Qualluviartuuq   Quebec   Queen Charlotte Islands   Quartz Lake   Queen Elizabeth

Resolute   Rankin Inlet   Reindeer Lake   Ross River   Rabbitskin River   Ramparts River   Red River   Rennie Lake   Resolution Island

Rae

Rat River

Raanes Peninsula

Rae

Richmond Gulf

Rainbow Lake

Rigolet

Rr

Two **rabbits**
sit
outside a
root cellar.

Reliance   Repulse Bay   Rancheria River   Raanes Peninsula   Rat River   Redstone River   Rigolet   Rainbow Lake   Richmond Gulf

Ss

The **sled** skims over the soft **snow.**

Tt

Trapper Tom
has three
frozen
trout.

Tanacross   Talkeetna   Teller   Tuktoyaktuk   Takhini   Tetlin   Tungsten   Telegraph Creek   Telkwa   Thompson   Tatlatui Lake

Taltson River

Takla Lake

Thelon River

Tatlatui Lake

Thompson

Teslin

Tagish

Thelon River   Takla Lake   Tanana   Togiak   Tok   Tasiujaq   Taltson River   Tagish   Teslin   Tetlin   Tungsten   Telegraph Creek

Uu

The constable in **uniform** likes my **uncle's** **ukulele.**

Vv

Vera
takes Victor
for a
vaccination.

Ww

The wet **walrus** watches the **whales.**

Xx

Excited
children dance
round the
Xmas tree.

We couldn't find a single northern place beginning with X. Do you know any? Here are some

We couldn't find a single northern place beginning with X.   Do you know any?   Here are some names with an X in them, though.

Yy

A young
Yukoner
yells beside the
Yukon River.

Do you know any more names beginning with Y?   Yathkyed Lake   Yelverton Bay

Lake Hazen

Tazin Lake

Kruzof Island

Mount Edziza

Spatsizi

Rae Edzo

Elizabeth

Zz

In zero weather
Zach makes a
zigzag path to the
zinc mine.

Here are a few more things in the pictures that begin with each letter. Can you add still more?

A airplane… aspen trees… ax

B bark… beaver… berries… birds… black

C campfire… cap… caribou… cat… clouds

D dandelions… dog… drum… drumstick

E eagle… electricity pole… ermine… evergreen

F firewood… forest… fuel

G game… geese… gun

H hats… hockey stick… hills… horse… house

I ice… icebergs… icicles… ice floes

J jackfish… jack rabbit… jawbone… jet plane

K kerosene stove… kettle… killer whale… kindling

L ladle… lake… lamp or lantern… lightning

M magpie… mittens… moon… mountains… mukluks

N noose… nuggets (of gold)

O oildrum… orange… outboard

P pack… pail… pan

Q quills (porcupine on mukluk)

R ravens… red… ridge… rifle… river

S sky… snowshoe… spruce tree… sun

T toboggan… toque… tree

U ulu… underwear

V valley… veterinarian… vixen

W water… waves

X xylophone

Y yellow

Z zipper

Ted Harrison

This is the second alphabet book Ted Harrison has created. The first called NORTHLAND ALPHABET was done for the Indian and Metis children he taught at the Wabasca, Alberta, reserve a year after he came to Canada. In it he drew animals, objects and scenes that would be familiar to them.

In A NORTHERN ALPHABET he has extended the range to cover peoples living across North America, north of the 60th parallel (although in a few cases he has gone as far south as the 55th). His first book was drawn in black and white; this one is in the fabulous color that has become his trademark as an artist. It is intended for all children of the North, regardless of race or ancestry, for adults who might be learning English, and for southern children who wonder what it is like to live through the northern year.

Ted was born in England in 1926, the son of a coal-miner. He studied art and art teaching at Hartlepool and Newcastle upon Tyne. After serving with the British Intelligence Corps in Africa, the Middle East and the Far East, he returned to England. He started teaching in 1951 and taught in Malaya and New Zealand before coming to Canada.

In 1968 he accepted a teaching post in Carcross and the Yukon has been his home and inspiration ever since. It was there he discarded almost everything he had learned in formal art training and started to interpret his surroundings in a new way, so distinctive, so colorful, so magical that once seen it is unforgettable. The honors he has received and the exhibitions of his paintings stretch from Alaska down and across Canada. His first children's book CHILDREN OF THE YUKON (1977) won several awards; he was the first Canadian artist to see his work accepted into the prestigious Illustrators' Exhibit in Bologna, Italy. Another book on the Yukon, THE LAST HORIZON, followed in 1980.